MIND BENDERS®
B1

DEDUCTIVE THINKING SKILLS

SERIES TITLES
Mind Benders®
Beginning Book 1 ▪ Book 2
Warm-Up
A1 ▪ A2 ▪ A3 ▪ A4
B1 ▪ B2 ▪ B3 ▪ B4
C1 ▪ C2 ▪ C3

ANITA HARNADEK

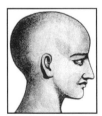

©2005, 2000, 1978
THE CRITICAL THINKING CO.™
www.CriticalThinking.com
Phone: 800-458-4849 Fax: 831-393-3277
P.O. Box 1610 • Seaside • CA 93955-1610
ISBN 978-0-89455-019-5

TABLE OF CONTENTS

TEACHER SUGGESTIONS

PURPOSE

Students with wide ranges of ability, motivation, and achievement seem to be remarkably attracted to *Mind Benders®* problems. Students think *Mind Benders®* are fun, not work. The purpose of the *Mind Benders®* series is to improve deductive reasoning, reading comprehension skills, and organized analysis skills.

GENERAL INFORMATION

There are fourteen exercise books in this series:

Mind Benders® Beginning BOOK 1

Mind Benders® Beginning BOOK 2

Mind Benders® Warm-Up

Mind Benders® A1

Mind Benders® A2

Mind Benders® A3

Mind Benders® A4

Mind Benders® B1

Mind Benders® B2

Mind Benders® B3

Mind Benders® B4

Mind Benders® C1

Mind Benders® C2

Mind Benders® C3

The **A** series is easy, **C** is difficult, and **B** is, clearly, in-between with medium level problems.

The Beginning level is the easiest level and is often used to introduce students (as young as preschool) to *Mind Benders®* problems and charts. *Mind Benders®* WARM UP (see listing of titles above) has easy problems with a handful of medium problems. This book is used to give auditory *Mind Benders®* to students.

Since some teachers will need more problems for their students than others, more than one book is available in each of the A, B, and C levels. Within a level, there is no substantial difference in difficulty between the books offered. (For example, a teacher who needs 15 problems at the "A" level may order any of the four *Mind Benders®* books in the A series.)

See page iv for general comments about assumptions that can be made from clues.

HELPFUL HINTS ABOUT SOLVING MIND BENDERS®

Most *Mind Benders®* in the Beginning, A, B, and C categories are solved more easily if a chart is used than if the solver simply makes notes about the clues given. To help students solve the problems, each *Mind Benders®* is accompanied by a chart made especially for that particular problem.

See page vi for a step-by-step explanation of how to use charts to solve *Mind Benders®* problems, including the way each chart looks after each step. None of the problems used there are used as exercises in any of the *Mind Benders®* books.

The instructions (in highly abbreviated form, of course) are these: To fill in a chart, make a notation in each square which is eliminated by a clue. (The notation might be the clue number or the word "no," for example.) When there is only one blank square left in a row (or column) within a category, then "X" that square. Then note the elimination of all the other squares in the matching column and row. When a chart contains three or more categories, then either the elimination of a square or the "X"ing of a square may also give you more information about previous clues. (For example, if you know that Mr. Brown owns the red car and you have just discovered that the Chevrolet is not the red car, then you have also discovered that Mr. Brown does not own the Chevrolet.)

SOLUTIONS

Note 1: Each problem has only one solution. If the notation used for eliminations is simply a "no," then the completed chart will have an "X" for each combination named in the solutions given below, and the chart will have a "no" everywhere else. If the notation used for elimination is a clue number, however, then the completed chart may vary from one student to another. (This is because eliminations can sometimes be made in different orders.)

Note 2: If your solutions do not agree with those given, refer to the Examples and Step-by-Step Procedures on page vii for information on how to use charts to solve *Mind Benders®* problems.

ABOUT THE CLUES IN Mind Benders®

In general, the *Mind Benders®* assume that you will, when using the clues, apply three guidelines unless a problem leads you to believe otherwise:

1. Think of everyday situations rather than of highly unusual exceptions.

2. Think of standards which are generally acceptable to U.S. society as a whole.

3. Use common sense and context in deciding what the clues mean.

Following are examples:

a. Assume that only males have male names (John, Robert, Dave) and only females have female names (Mary, Jennifer, Cathy), but be careful not to make such assumptions about unisex names (Pat, Chris).

b. Assume that typical U.S. social relationships apply. For example, if John is engaged to Mary, you may assume that they know each other. You may assume that very close relatives know each other.

c. Don't assume that rare age relationships may apply. For example, don't assume that a 7 year old might be a college graduate, or that a parent might be younger than his or her adopted child. On the other hand, although most cases of age may be in one direction, enough cases in the other direction may exist so that these would not be considered especially unusual. For example, a husband may be a good deal younger than his wife, or a 45 year old may get the mumps.

d. Assume that animals are of normal size. For example, "a horse" is not "a pygmy horse"; "a small dog" is smaller than a goat; a "large dog" is simply one of the larger breeds of dogs. If a problem talks about a cat and a fox, assume that the cat is smaller than the fox. Do not think that maybe the cat is fully grown and the fox is a few weeks old.

e. Assume that animals are called by their usual names within the context. For example, if John and Mary have a pet dog and a pet cat, assume that the cat is an ordinary household cat, rather than maybe a tiger or a leopard.

f. Don't look for tricky situations. For example, suppose that the problem has four houses in a row (and no other houses), and suppose that Debby lives next door to Gary. Don't assume that Debby or Gary might live in a garage between two of the houses. That is, assume that they live in two of the four houses in the problem.

g. Assume that typical U.S. social situations apply. For example, if John went on a date with Abbott, assume two things: (1) Abbott is a female; (2) neither John nor Abbott is married, since (a) when a married couple goes out, we do not call it a "date," and (b) if either one is married to someone else, then it is not typical for him or her to be dating someone.

h. Pay attention to what the clues say. For example, suppose that a problem has four people, and suppose that one clue says, "Cathy and the dentist ride to work together in a car pool." Also suppose that another clue says, "Brown, who does not know any of the other three people, is not the typist." Then you should deduce that neither Cathy nor the dentist is Brown.

i. Exact wording to eliminate ambiguities sometimes makes a clue too long. The clue is then shortened to the point where it is unambiguous to most people, but some people would still recognize ambiguities and object to the wording. In such cases, consider the context and the intent of the clue. As examples:

(1) "Neither Bob nor Young lives in the white house," means, "Bob is not Young, and Bob does not live in the white house, and Young does not live in the white house."

(2) "John and Abbott went bowling with Dave and Smith," means, "Four different people went bowling together. One of these was John, one was Abbott, one was Dave, and one was Smith."

(3) "Jane doesn't know either Mary or the artist," means, "Jane doesn't know Mary, and Jane doesn't know the artist, and Mary is not the artist."

(4) "Neither Carol nor Bill went to the party, and Norris didn't go, either," refers to three different people.

(5) In general, "neither ... nor" and "either ... or" sentences will refer to separate things, as in the above examples. Just plain "or" sentences, however, are sometimes less definite, as in this example: "Neither Becky nor Jackson has the dog or is the secretary." Here, Becky and Jackson are different people, but we aren't sure that the person who has the dog is not also the secretary.

HOW TO USE A CHART

A *Mind Benders®* problem gives you two or more lists of things and asks you to match each item in one list with an item in the other list. Finding answers is easier if a chart is made showing all the lists at once and is then filled in. For more detailed examples, see page vii.

Note that the number of small boxes (within a large box) is the square of the number of things in any one list (Example 1 has three things in each list, so each large box has 9 small boxes).

EXAMPLE of a TWO-DIMENSIONAL PROBLEM

Davis, Edwards, and Jones are an astronaut, a computer programmer, and a skin diver.

1.   Davis is not the astronaut or the computer programmer.

2.   Jones is not the astronaut.

What does each person do?

Solution:

Make a chart and use clue 1—put "no" in D/A and D/CP. This leaves only one blank space in the "D" row. Write X to show that Davis is the skin diver.

Since we know that Davis is the skin diver, we can fill in the other spaces in the "SD" column. Write "no" for both Edwards and Jones.

We are through with the first clue, so now we can use the second clue. Write "no" in J/A to show Jones is not the astronaut.

The "A" column now has only one blank space, so we X it to show that Edwards is the astronaut. (The "J" row also has only one blank space, but it is a good idea to work on only one row or column at a time.)

The "E" row has only one remaining blank space, so we write "no" (since Edwards is the astronaut, he is not the computer programmer).

In the "J" row, one space remains, so we X it (Jones is the programmer).

The chart now shows the solution: Davis is the skin diver, Edwards is the astronaut, and Jones is the computer programmer.

	A	CP	SD
D	no	no	X
E			
J			

	A	CP	SD
D	no	no	X
E			no
J			no

	A	CP	SD
D	no	no	X
E			no
J	no		no

	A	CP	SD
D	no	no	X
E	X		no
J	no		no

	A	CP	SD
D	no	no	X
E	X	no	no
J	no		no

	A	CP	SD
D	no	no	X
E	X	no	no
J	no	X	no

EXAMPLES AND STEP-BY-STEP PROCEDURES

THREE-DIMENSIONAL PROBLEMS

To solve a three-dimensional problem, we make the chart so that each item in each list can be compared with each item in both other lists.

EXAMPLE 1

Problem: Davis, Edwards, and Farman are an astronaut, a bookbinder, and a skin diver. Their ages are 25, 30, and 35. Match each person's name, job, and age.

1. Davis is younger than the astronaut but older than Farman.

2. The skin diver is younger than the bookbinder.

Solution: To help keep our thinking straight on clue 1, we'll write in mathematical symbols: F < D < A. Then Farman is the youngest, Davis is in the middle, and the astronaut is the oldest. So Farman is 25, Davis is 30, and the astronaut is 35.

It is important to notice here that if the puzzle involved four people instead of three, we could not say that Farman is the youngest or that the astronaut is the oldest. The most we could say is (1) Farman is not either of the two oldest people, (2) Davis is not either the oldest or the youngest person, and (3) the astronaut is not either of the two youngest people. Let's look at how the chart works for this kind of problem.

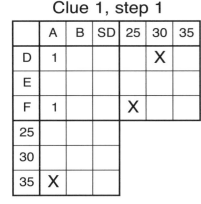

Clue 1, step 1

	A	B	SD	25	30	35
D	1				X	
E						
F	1			X		
25						
30						
35	X					

Clue 1, step 2

	A	B	SD	25	30	35
D	1			25	X	D
E				25	30	
F	1			X	F	F
25	A					
30	A					
35	X	35	35			

Clue 1, step 3

	A	B	SD	25	30	35
D	1			25	X	D
E	X	E	E	25	30	X
F	1			X	F	F
25	A					
30	A					
35	X	35	35			

Clue 2 says the skin diver is younger than the bookbinder. The chart (from clue 1, step 3) says that Edwards, the astronaut, is 35. This leaves ages 25 and 30. So the skin diver is 25 and the bookbinder is 30. But we know from the chart that Farman is 25 and Davis is 30. So Farman is the skin diver and Davis is the bookbinder.

	A	B	SD	25	30	35
D	1	X	SD	25	X	D
E	X	E	E	25	30	X
F	1	F	X	X	F	F
25	A	25	X			
30	A	X	SD			
35	X	35	35			

Solution: Davis, bookbinder, 30; Edwards, astronaut, 35; Farman, skin diver, 25.

EXAMPLE 2

Problem: Davis, Edwards, Farman, and Gurley are an astronaut, a bookbinder, a plumber, and a skin diver. Their first names are Harold, Jenny, Ken, and Laura. Match up each person's full name and job.

1. Farman and the astronaut joined the same fraternity in college.

2. Edwards said she'd teach Jenny how to swim.

3. Ken asked the plumber if he could install a solar heating system for him.

4. Davis enjoys her work.

Solution: (Can you solve this one before reading the solution below?)

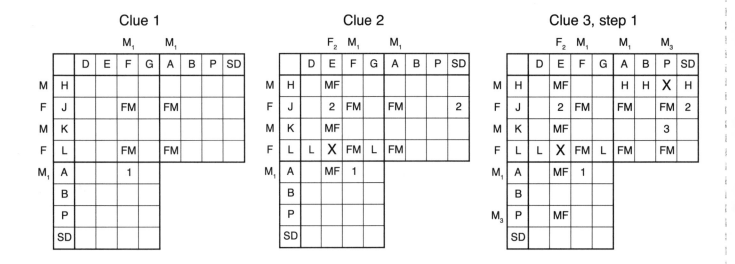

Clue 1

		D	E	F	G	A	B	P	SD
M	H								
F	J			FM		FM			
M	K								
F	L			FM		FM			
M₁	A				1				
	B								
	P								
	SD								

(top markers: M₁ above F, M₁ above A)

Clue 2

		D	E	F	G	A	B	P	SD
M	H		MF						
F	J		2	FM		FM			2
M	K		MF						
F	L	L	X	FM	L	FM			
M₁	A		MF	1					
	B								
	P								
	SD								

(top markers: F₂ above E, M₁ above F, M₁ above A)

Clue 3, step 1

		D	E	F	G	A	B	P	SD
M	H		MF			H	H	X	H
F	J		2	FM		FM		FM	2
M	K		MF					3	
F	L	L	X	FM	L	FM		FM	
M₁	A		MF	1					
	B								
M₃	P		MF						
	SD								

(top markers: F₂ above E, M₁ above F, M₁ above A, M₃ above P)

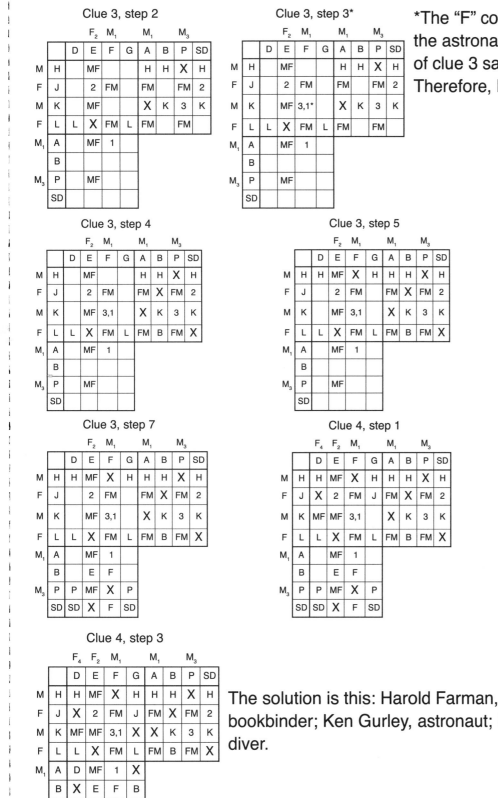

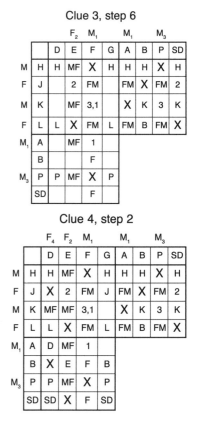

*The "F" column says Farman is not the astronaut (clue 1). But step 2 of clue 3 says Ken is the astronaut. Therefore, Ken is not Farman.

The solution is this: Harold Farman, plumber; Jenny Davis, bookbinder; Ken Gurley, astronaut; Laura Edwards, skin diver.

Here's one more three-dimensional puzzle for you to try before we go on to a four-dimensional puzzle.

EXAMPLE 3

Problem: Harold, Jenny, Ken, and Laura are 12, 16, 20, and 25 years old. Their last names are Davis, Edwards, Farman, and Gurley. Find each person's full name and age.

1. Harold's and Gurley's ages are perfect squares.

2. Edwards is Jenny's older sister.

3. Farman is younger than Ken but older than Edwards' sister.

Solution: Clue 1: (a) Harold is not Gurley. (b) The only perfect squares listed are 16 and 25, so neither Harold nor Gurley is 12 or 20.

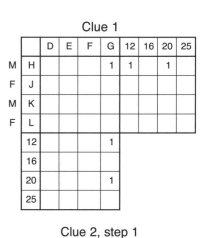

Clue 1

		D	E	F	G	12	16	20	25
M	H					1	1		1
F	J								
M	K								
F	L								
	12			1					
	16								
	20			1					
	25								

Clue 2, step 1: (a) Edwards is a female and is not Jenny. So Edwards is Laura. (b) From clue 1, the ages of 16 and 25 are taken by Ken and Gurley, and Laura Edwards is neither of these people. So she is either 12 or 20. But she is older than Jenny, so she cannot be the youngest person, 12. So Laura Edwards is 20.

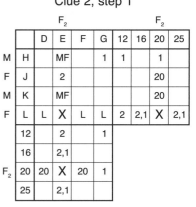

Clue 2, step 1

		D	E	F	G	12	16	20	25
M	H		MF			1	1		1
F	J		2					20	
M	K		MF					20	
F	L	L	X	L	L	2	2,1	X	2,1
	12		2		1				
	16		2,1						
F₂	20	20	X	20		1			
	25		2,1						

Clue 2, step 2: (a) Laura Edwards is 20 and is older than Jenny, so Jenny is either 12 or 16. (b) So neither Jenny nor Laura is 25. Then the 25 year old is a male.

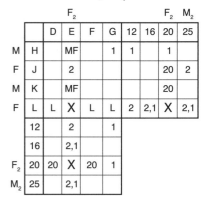

Clue 2, step 2

		D	E	F	G	12	16	20	25
M	H		MF			1	1		1
F	J		2					20	2
M	K		MF					20	
F	L	L	X	L	L	2	2,1	X	2,1
	12		2		1				
	16		2,1						
F₂	20	20	X	20		1			
M₂	25		2,1						

Clue 3, step 1: Edwards' sister is Jenny (clue 2), so Farman is younger than Ken but older than Jenny. In mathematical notation, $J < F < K$. Laura Edwards, 20, is not Jenny or Farman or Ken, so the only ages left are 12, 16, and 25. So Jenny is 12, Farman is 16, and Ken is 25.

Clue 3, step 1

		D	E	F	G	12	16	20 F_2	25 M_2
M	H		MF		1	1		1	25
F	J		2			X	J	20	2
M	K		MF			12	K	20	X
F	L	L	X	L	L	2	2,1	X	2,1
	12		2	F	1				
	16	16	2,1	X	16				
F_2	20	20	X	20	1				
M_2	25		2,1	F					

Clue 3, step 2: We look for remaining spaces we are forced to X, and we X them.

Clue 3, step 2

		D	E	F	G	12	16	20 F_2	25 M_2
M	H		MF		1	1	X	1	25
F	J		2			X	J	20	2
M	K		MF			12	K	20	X
F	L	L	X	L	L	2	2,1	X	2,1
	12	X	2	F	1				
	16	16	2,1	X	16				
F_2	20	20	X	20	1				
M_2	25	D	2,1	F	X				

Clue 3, step 3: (a) The chart shows that Harold and Farman are both 16, so Harold is Farman. (b) Jenny and Davis are both 12, so Jenny is Davis. (c) Only the K/G space is left. Since Ken and Gurley are both 25, we X this space.

Clue 3, step 3

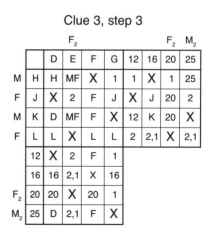

		D	E	F	G	12	16	20 F_2	25 M_2
M	H	H	MF	X	1	1	X	1	25
F	J	X	2	F	J	X	J	20	2
M	K	D	MF	F	X	12	K	20	X
F	L	L	X	L	L	2	2,1	X	2,1
	12	X	2	F	1				
	16	16	2,1	X	16				
F_2	20	20	X	20	1				
M_2	25	D	2,1	F	X				

So the solution is this: Harold Farman, 16; Jenny Davis, 12; Ken Gurley, 25; Laura Edwards, 20.

FOUR- AND FIVE-DIMENSIONAL PROBLEMS

A problem of four or more dimensions is solved the same way as the others. Again, the chart must be made so that each list can be compared with all the other lists.

EXAMPLE 4

Problem: Davis, Edwards, and Gurley are the first, second, and third basemen for the Detroit Tigers. Their first names are Harold, José, and Ken. Their ages are 23, 25, and 28. From the clues below, match up everything.

1. The second baseman has a higher batting average than Ken or Davis.

2. The first baseman is younger than Edwards and older than Ken.

3. José and Davis ate pizza with some of the rest of the team after yesterday's game.

Solution:

Clue 1

	D	E	G	1st	2nd	3rd	23	25	28
H									
J									
K	1				1				
1st									
2nd	1								
3rd									
23									
25									
28									

Clue 2, step 1

(K < 1st < E)

	D	E	G	1st	2nd	3rd	23	25	28
H			G			3rd	23		
J			G			3rd	23		
K	1	2	X	2	1	X	X	2	2
1st		2							
2nd	1								
3rd									
23		2		2					
25		2		X	25	25			
28	28	X		28	2				

Clue 2, step 2 (Gurley is Ken, so post facts about Ken in Gurley's column. Also match "3rd" and "23.")

	D	E	G	1st	2nd	3rd	23	25	28
H			G			3rd	23		
J			G			3rd	23		
K	1	2	X	2	1	X	X	2	2
1st		2	K						
2nd	1		K						
3rd	3rd	3rd	X						
23	23	2	X	2	23	X			
25		2	K	X	25	25			
28	28	X	28	2		3rd			

Clue 2, step 3

	D	E	G	1st	2nd	3rd	23	25	28
H			G			3rd	23		
J			G			3rd	23		
K	1	2	X	2	1	X	X	2	2
1st	X	2	K						
2nd	1	X	K						
3rd	3rd	3rd	X						
23	23	2	X	2	23	X			
25	X	2	K	X	25	25			
28	28	X	28	2	X	3rd			

Clue 3, step 1

	D	E	G	1st	2nd	3rd	23	25	28
H	X	H	G			3rd	23		
J	3	X	G			3rd	23		
K	1	2	X	2	1	X	X	2	2
1st	X	2	K						
2nd	1	X	K						
3rd	3rd	3rd	X						
23	23	2	X	2	23	X			
25	X	2	K	X	25	25			
28	28	X	28	2	X	3rd			

The rest of the entries are now forced, so the chart is left for you to complete.

The solution is this: Harold Davis, first baseman, 25; José Edwards, second baseman, 28; Ken Gurley, third baseman, 23.

The preceding problem gave us four lists of things to match up (first names, last names, positions, and ages), and so it is called a four-dimensional problem. A general chart for a four-dimensional problem would look like the one at the right.

	headings for second list	headings for third list	headings for fourth list
headings for first list	small boxes	small boxes	small boxes
headings for third list	small boxes		
headings for fourth list	small boxes	small boxes	

A general chart for a five-dimensional problem (a problem with five lists of things to match up) would look like the one at the right.

	headings for second list	headings for third list	headings for fourth list	headings for fifth list
headings for first list	small boxes	small boxes	small boxes	small boxes
headings for third list	small boxes			
headings for fourth list	small boxes	small boxes		
headings for fifth list	small boxes	small boxes	small boxes	

1. Who Works Where?

Klare, Lemon, Morton, and Nelson are women who love their work (dress designer, florist, gardener, and symphony conductor). From the clues below, match up each woman's name with her kind of work.

1. Klare is violently allergic to most plants.

2. Lemon and the florist are roommates.

3. Lemon likes only rock music.

4. The gardener, the dress designer, and Nelson are strangers.

Chart for Problem 1

	dress designer	florist	gardener	symphony conductor
Klare				
Lemon				
Morton				
Nelson				

2. Around the World

André, Barney, Cleo, and Dixie, whose last names are North, Olsen, Partin, and Ryan, live in Egypt, France, India, and Mexico. Use the clues below to match up everything.

1. Cleo, North, and the Indian are pen pals.

2. Ryan has never written to any of the other three people.

3. The Frenchman wants to meet André.

4. Olsen and the Indian talked to each other on the telephone.

5. The Mexican woman saw Dixie's picture in the paper.

6. André is not the Egyptian.

7. Dixie is not North.

Chart for Problem 2

	North	Olsen	Partin	Ryan	Egypt	France	India	Mexico
André								
Barney								
Cleo								
Dixie								
Egypt								
France								
India								
Mexico								

3.　Each Has Two Jobs

Roberta, Steve, Thelma, and Vince each have two jobs. Listed alphabetically, the jobs are chef, nurse, police officer, professional wrestler, security guard, teacher, telephone operator, and waiter.

Use the clues below to figure out each person's two jobs.

1. Roberta, the chef, and the police officer all went golfing together.

2. Vince never had any education past the ninth grade.

3. The nurse was assigned to desk duty when he sprained his ankle.

4. The chef's husband is the telephone operator.

5. Roberta is not the professional wrestler.

Chart for Problem 3

	Roberta	Steve	Thelma	Vince
chef				
nurse				
police officer				
professional wrestler				
security guard				
teacher				
telephone operator				
waiter				

4.   At the Court

A count, a duke, an earl, and a knight were discussing the nation's problems with the king. Their names were Royal, Silverton, Towman, Uppercrust, and Vincent.

From the clues below, match the name of each man with his title.

1. "The peasants are very troublesome," Royal said.

2. "Yes," Towman agreed, "but we might be, too, if we were as poor as they."

3. "You're both wrong, of course," said the king. "I don't find them to be troublesome at all."

4. "Oh, I didn't mean that they cause trouble," the duke corrected himself. The man who had agreed with him nodded.

5. "Aha! Fence-straddling as usual," the knight thought. "Let's see them get out of this one."

6. Vincent, trying to prevent an argument, said, "Your Highness, I think that Royal and the count meant that the poverty of the peasants distresses them, not that the peasants try to cause trouble."

7. Disappointed, but not wanting to seem to be disagreeable, Uppercrust said, "Yes, I'm sure that's what they meant, Your Highness."

Chart for Problem 4

	Royal	Silverton	Towman	Uppercrust	Vincent
count					
duke					
earl					
king					
knight					

5. Armed Forces

The last names of Fernando, Helena, and Jennifer are Grayson, Kraft, and Landers. Each person joined a branch of the U.S. armed forces—army, marines, or navy.

Find each person's full name and armed service branch.

1. Landers is not a marine.

2. Grayson likes being in the army and tried unsuccessfully to talk Helena into joining.

3. The marine said he didn't like the basic training.

Chart for Problem 5

	Grayson	Kraft	Landers	army	marines	navy
Fernando						
Helena						
Jennifer						
army						
marines						
navy						

6. Science Fair

Edith, Francine, Hector, and Igor placed first, second, third, and fourth in the science fair. Their last names are Amwell, Boswell, Cross, and Drake.

Find each person's full name and science fair rank.

1. Boswell said she'd have ranked higher if she had worked harder on her project.

2. Igor ranked higher than Drake but lower than Francine.

3. Cross's father said he was proud of her for her fine project.

4. Edith ranked lower than Amwell.

5. Hector did not rank third.

© 2000 The Critical Thinking Co.™ • www.CriticalThinking.com • 800-458-4849

Chart for Problem 6

	Amwell	Boswell	Cross	Drake	1st	2nd	3rd	4th
Edith								
Francine								
Hector								
Igor								
1st				
2nd				
3rd				
4th				

7. Part-time Jobs

Jeanette, Marcia, Saralee, and Theodora all hold part-time jobs after school. The jobs are carpenter's apprentice, cook, delivery person for a pizzeria, and paper girl. Each person uses part of her earnings to pay for a telephone at home. The telephone colors are blue, green, ivory, and white.

Find each person's job and telephone color.

1. The carpenter's apprentice and the person with the white telephone live on a street which is two blocks away from the street where Saralee and the person with the green telephone live.

2. Jeanette and the cook live next door to each other, but Marcia and the delivery person live two doors away from each other.

3. Theodora lives on the same street as the person with the ivory telephone.

4. The cook does not have the white telephone.

Chart for Problem 7

	carpenter's apprentice	cook	delivery person	paper route	blue	green	ivory	white
Jeanette								
Marcia								
Saralee								
Theodora								
blue				
green				
ivory				
white				

8. In the Army

Two women and two men (Ann, Brett, Dje-Da, and Eliza) are in the army. Their ranks, from lowest to highest, are corporal, sergeant, first lieutenant, and major. Their last names are Hunt, Jackson, Paul, and Younger.

Find each person's full name and rank.

1. There are a total of six syllables in each person's full name and rank.

2. The first lieutenant likes her life in the army.

3. Hunt has a lower rank than Younger but a higher rank than Paul.

Chart for Problem 8

	Hunt	Jackson	Paul	Younger	corporal	first lieutenant	major	sergeant
Ann								
Brett								
Dje-Da								
Eliza								
corporal								
lieutenant								
major								
sergeant								

9. Pets at Home

Four children (Ed, Marie, Natalie, and Quentin) are different ages (9, 10, 11, and 13), have different pets (cat, dog, gerbil, and parakeet), and live in different kinds of houses (aluminum siding, brick, frame, and stucco). From the clues below, see if you can find each child's name, age, pet, and kind of house.

1. Ed and the cat's owner play on the same team in Little League baseball.

2. Marie and the gerbil's owner live next door to each other.

3. The dog owner is two years older than the girl who lives in the house with aluminum siding.

4. The 11-year-old lives a block away from Quentin, who does not live in the frame house.

5. The parakeet owner's parents won't let her play football.

6. The brick house is two blocks from the 9-year-old's house.

7. Natalie, Marie, and the 11-year-old sometimes walk to school together.

8. The 10-year-old is a girl.

9. The cat owner is younger than the person who lives in the stucco house but is older than Marie.

Chart for Problem 9

	9	10	11	13	cat	dog	gerbil	parakeet	aluminum siding	brick	frame	stucco
Ed												
Marie												
Natalie												
Quentin												
cat												
dog												
gerbil												
parakeet												
aluminum siding												
brick												
frame												
stucco												

10. Baseball Players

Ergen, Flore, Gruman, and Haller each play a different position (first base, second base, third base, and shortstop) on a baseball team. The first names of the men are Alton, Brian, Carlton, and Delbert.

Read the clues below and match up everything.

1. Alton, Ergen, and the third baseman had lunch together today.

2. Brian and Gruman are married, but the men who play second and third bases are single.

3. Haller and Delbert each got four hits in yesterday's game.

4. Carlton's wife invited the first baseman's wife to watch the game with her today.

Chart for Problem 10

	Ergen	Flore	Gruman	Haller	first base	second base	third base	shortstop
Alton								
Brian								
Carlton								
Delbert								
first base								
second base								
third base								
shortstop								

11. The Jobs People Do

Karen, Laura, Manuel, and Nevin are a carpenter, a firefighter, a jockey, and a soldier (U.S. Army career person). Their last names are Orton, Pauling, Quintil, and Ruter.

Read the statements below and see if you can match up everything.

1. Manuel, who should weigh about 190 pounds but weighs 250 pounds, has been on a low carbohydrate diet for the past two weeks.

2. Pauling has one of the two most dangerous jobs.

3. Karen doesn't wear a uniform while working.

4. Quintil eats like a pig, but her small size and her natural ability for her job make her in great demand.

5. Orton and Karen split a large pizza last night.

6. Nevin is not the firefighter.

Chart for Problem 11

	Orton	Pauling	Quintil	Ruter	carpenter	firefighter	jockey	soldier
Karen								
Laura								
Manuel								
Nevin								
carpenter								
firefighter								
jockey								
soldier								

12. Pen Pals

Six pairs of people are pen pals. From the information below, see if you can find each person's first name, last name, and country, as well as the first and last names and country of each person's pen pal.

1. The first names of the twelve people are Andy, Bob, Carol, Dolly, Everett, Freda, Gwen, Holly, Ida, Jack, Ken, and Lance.

2. The last names of the twelve people are Mancel, Nasker, Ordphin, Pastury, Quinthe, Roth, Skycard, Thompson, Urskel, Vander, Wildpoy, and Yerkel.

3. Two people live in Australia. The other ten live in Brazil, Canada, China, Egypt, India, Kenya, Mexico, Peru, Poland, and Spain.

4. The first and last names of each person have no letters in common.

5. The name of each person's country has exactly four letters in common with the person's full name (first and last combined, with no letter counted more than once).

6. No pair of pen pals is the same sex.

7. No pair of pen pals both live in the Americas.

8. One Australian's pen pal is an African, and the other Australian's pen pal is a European.

9. The pen pal of one of the Europeans is a North American.

10. Jack is not Carol's pen pal.

11. Andy and Ida are not pen pals.

Charts for Problem 12

	Mancel	Nasker	Ordphin	Pastury	Quinthe	Roth	Skycard	Thompson	Urskel	Vander	Wildpoy	Yerkel
Andy												
Bob												
Carol												
Dolly												
Everett												
Freda												
Gwen												
Holly												
Ida												
Jack												
Ken												
Lance												
Australia												
Australia												
Brazil												
Canada												
China												
Egypt												
India												
Kenya												
Mexico												
Peru												
Poland												
Spain												

	Australia	Australia	Brazil	Canada	Kenya	Spain
China						
Egypt						
India						
Mexico						
Peru						
Poland						

13. Their Favorite Things

Ada, Brian, Carmella, and Daniel live in Maine, Nebraska, Oregon, and Pennsylvania. Their last names are Eaton, Farmer, Grey, and Hill. Their favorite foods are Idaho potatoes, jam, kidney beans, and lemon pie. Their favorite colors are red, salmon, tan, and umber.

Find each person's name, favorite food, favorite color, and state.

1. Ada and Eaton live in the East.

2. Hill and Carmella don't like sweet foods.

3. Daniel and Farmer don't like brownish colors.

4. The man who lives in Maine went to school with Brian.

5. The Nebraskan doesn't like reddish colors.

6. Hill's favorite color doesn't have any of the same letters as her full name.

7. Carmella doesn't like red, but that's the lemon pie eater's favorite color.

8. Eaton's favorite food is not lemon pie.

9. The kidney bean eater does not live in Nebraska.

Chart for Problem 13

	Eaton	Farmer	Grey	Hill	Idaho potatoes	jam	kidney beans	lemon pie	ME	NB	OR	PA	red	salmon	tan	umber
Ada																
Brian																
Carmella																
Daniel																
Idaho potatoes																
jam																
kidney beans																
lemon pie																
ME																
NB																
OR																
PA																
red																
salmon																
tan																
umber																

14. Names and Jobs

From the statements that follow, find the first name, last name, and occupation of each person. (One of these people is Leon.)

1. Packard and the computer operator were ushers at a wedding.

2. Kizzy and Monty told the toolmaker that she was conceited.

3. The firefighter and the computer operator are engaged.

4. Quill had her ears pierced last week.

5. Monty and the nurse are good friends.

6. Richards likes her occupation, but she thinks Julie's is safer.

Chart for Problem 14

	Quill	Packard	Richards	Smith	computer operator	firefighter	nurse	toolmaker
Julie								
Kizzy								
Leon								
Monty								
computer operator								
firefighter								
nurse								
toolmaker								

28

SOLUTIONS

GENERAL COMMENTS ABOUT SOLUTIONS

There is more than one way to approach the solution of most Mind Benders®. For example, if a problem has five clues, you might choose to apply clue 4 first and clue 2 second, while the solution here for that problem uses clue 3 first and clue 5 second. Since there is only one final answer to the problem, the order in which the clues are used does not affect the final answer.

In order to understand a solution here, it is necessary that you have a copy of the problem to refer to while you are reading the solution. Also, it is definitely suggested, particularly for the problems in the B and C series, that you write down the findings as you go through a solution in order to help keep track of the rationale. For example, suppose a problem uses first and last names and occupations of three people. Before you start reading the solution here, write down the first names, leaving space to fill in the last names and occupations:

Bernard

Catherine

Donald

Then this is what your notes will look like as you read through (part of) the detailed solution, "Smith is a man (2) but isn't Donald (4), so he is Bernard."

Bernard Smith

Catherine

Donald

"The TV repairer is a man (3) but isn't Smith (3), so he is Donald."

Bernard Smith

Catherine

Donald,   TV repairer

Notice in the above example that clue numbers are referred to in parentheses.

DETAILED SOLUTIONS

1.

NAME	WORK
Klare	dress designer
Lemon	gardener
Morton	florist
Nelson	symphony conductor

Lemon is not the florist (2) or the symphony conductor (3), so she is either the gardener or the dress designer. Then she doesn't know Nelson (4), so Nelson is not her roommate, the florist (2). Nelson is not the gardener or the dress designer (4), so Nelson is the symphony conductor.

Klare is not the florist or the gardener (1), so she is the dress designer. Lemon isn't the florist (2), so she is the gardener. Then Morton is the florist.

2.

NAME	COUNTRY
André Partin	India
Barney North	France
Cleo Olsen	Mexico
Dixie Ryan	Egypt

The person living in Mexico is female (5) but isn't Dixie (5), so she is Cleo. The person living in France is male (3) but isn't André (3), so he is Barney. André doesn't live in Egypt (6), so Dixie does, and André lives in India.

North is not Cleo (1), André (1, India), or Dixie (7), so North is Barney. Three of the people write to each other (1), but Ryan is not one of these people (2), so Ryan is not Cleo (1) or André (1, India). So Ryan is Dixie. André (India) is not Olsen (4), so Cleo is, and André is Partin.

3.

NAME	JOB 1	JOB 2
Roberta	security guard	teacher
Steve	nurse	police officer
Thelma	chef	professional wrestler
Vince	telephone operator	waiter

The nurse is a man (3) but isn't Vince (2), so he is Steve. The chef is a woman (4) but isn't Roberta (1), so she is Thelma. Then Thelma (chef) isn't the police officer (1), and neither is Roberta (1) or Vince (2), so Steve is the police officer.

Steve's two occupations are now accounted for, so the other two male occupations that must be held by men are Vince's. These are the telephone operator (4, male) and the waiter (male, since "waitress" would be female).

Now both men's occupations are accounted for, so the remaining occupations are the women's. Roberta is not the professional wrestler (5), so Thelma is. Then Roberta's two occupations are security guard and teacher.

4.

NAME	TITLE
Royal	duke
Silverton	king
Towman	count
Uppercrust	knight
Vincent	earl

Royal and Towman are the duke and the count (1, 2, 4, 6). Royal is not the count (6), so Towman is, and so Royal is the duke. The king is not Uppercrust (7) or Vincent (6), so he is Silverton. The knight is willing to let Royal and Towman get out of trouble by themselves (5), but Vincent isn't (6), so Vincent isn't the knight. Then Vincent is the earl, and Uppercrust is the knight.

5.

FIRST NAME	LAST NAME	BRANCH
Fernando	Kraft	marines
Helena	Landers	navy
Jennifer	Grayson	army

The marine is a man (3), so he is Fernando. Helena is not in the army (2), so she is in the navy, and Jennifer is in the army. Then Jennifer is Grayson (2). Landers is not Fernando (1, marine), so Landers is Helena, and Fernando is Kraft.

6.

FIRST NAME	LAST NAME	PLACE
Edith	Boswell	third
Francine	Cross	first
Hector	Drake	fourth
Igor	Amwell	second

Boswell (1) and Cross (3) are girls, so Amwell and Drake are boys. Igor is not Drake (2), so he is Amwell. Then Hector is Drake.

From clue 2, a partial ordering

of the standings (high to low) is: Francine, Igor Amwell, Hector Drake. Igor Amwell's standing was higher than Edith's (4), so Francine had first place and Igor had second place. Hector didn't place third (5), so Edith did, and Hector placed fourth. Francine (first place) isn't Boswell (1), so Edith is, and Francine is Cross.

7.

NAME	JOB	TELEPHONE COLOR
Jeanette	paper route	green
Marcia	carpenter's apprentice	ivory
Saralee	cook	blue
Theodora	delivery person	white

Two of the girls live on one street, and the other two live on another street (1). One of these pairs of girls are the carpenter's apprentice and the person with the white telephone (1). Jeanette and the cook are also one of these pairs (2), but they are not the same pair, since the cook neither has the white telephone (4) nor is the carpenter's apprentice. Then Jeanette and the cook are the other pair in clue 1—that is, they are Saralee and the person with the green telephone. Jeanette isn't Saralee, so she has the green telephone, and so Saralee is the cook.

Then the carpenter's apprentice and the person with the white telephone (1) are also Marcia and the delivery person (2). The carpenter's apprentice isn't the delivery person, so she is Marcia. Then the delivery person has the white telephone. The delivery person is not Jeanette (green telephone), Marcia (2), or Saralee (cook), so she is Theodora. Then Marcia, who lives on the same street as Theodora (2), has the ivory telephone (3). This leaves Saralee with the blue telephone and Jeanette with the paper route.

8.

FIRST NAME	LAST NAME	RANK
Ann	Hunt	lieutenant
Brett	Jackson	corporal
Dje-Da	Younger	major
Eliza	Paul	sergeant

The lieutenant is a woman (2) but is not Eliza (1), so she is Ann. Since no last name has more than two syllables, Brett is the corporal (1). Then Brett is either Jackson or Younger (1). He isn't Younger (3, corporal), so he is Jackson. Since Dje-Da is either a sergeant or a major, his last name has two syllables (1), so he is not Hunt or Paul. Then Dje-Da is Younger. Younger is not a sergeant (3), so he is a major. This makes Eliza the sergeant. Paul isn't Amy (3, lieutenant), so she is Eliza, and Amy is Hunt.

9.

NAME	AGE	PET	HOUSE
Ed	11	dog	frame
Marie	9	parakeet	aluminum siding
Natalie	10	cat	brick
Quentin	13	gerbil	stucco

The 11-year-old is not Marie or Natalie (7) or Quentin (4), so he is Ed. The owner of the cat is not 9 or 13 (9) or 11 (1, Ed), so he or she is 10. Then Marie is 9 (9). The cat is owned by a girl (8) but not by Marie (9), so Natalie owns the cat. Then Quentin is 13. The parakeet is owned by a girl (5), so Marie has the parakeet. The girls are 9 and 10, so the dog owner has to be 11 (3), and Marie, 9 years old, lives in the house with aluminum siding (3). Quentin is left to own the gerbil. Then Quentin lives next door to Marie (2), so he doesn't live in the brick house (6, Marie is 9 years old) or the frame house (4), so he lives in the stucco house. Ed, 11 years old, lives a block away from Quentin (4), who lives next door to Marie (2), so Ed doesn't live in the brick house (6). Then Natalie lives in the brick house, and Ed lives in the frame house.

10.

FIRST NAME	LAST NAME	POSITION
Alton	Haller	second base
Brian	Ergen	first base
Carlton	Gruman	shortstop
Delbert	Flore	third base

The second and third basemen are single, while the first baseman and the shortstop are married (2). Carlton is married (4), but he isn't the first baseman (4), so Carlton is the shortstop. Brian is the first baseman (4, 2), and Carlton is Gruman (4, 2). Alton is not the third baseman (1), so he is the second baseman, and Delbert plays third base. Delbert is not Ergen (1, third base) or Haller (3), so he is Flore. Alton is not Ergen (1), so Brian is, and Alton is Haller.

11.

FIRST NAME	LAST NAME	JOB
Karen	Ruter	carpenter
Laura	Quintil	jockey
Manuel	Pauling	firefighter
Nevin	Orton	soldier

Karen is the carpenter (3), since the other three jobs require uniforms. Quintil is the jockey (4), since a small size is not necessarily an asset for the other jobs but it is for a jockey. Quintil is a woman (4) but she isn't Karen (carpenter), so she is Laura. Karen isn't Orton (5) or Pauling (2), so she is Ruter. Manuel isn't Orton (1, 5), so he is Pauling, and Nevin is Orton. Nevin isn't the firefighter (6), so Manuel is, and so Nevin is the soldier.

12.

FIRST NAME	LAST NAME	COUNTRY	PEN PAL'S FIRST NAME	PEN PAL'S LAST NAME	PEN PAL'S COUNTRY
Andy	Urskel	Poland	Dolly	Nasker	Australia
Bob	Mancel	Mexico	Freda	Thompson	Spain
Everett	Wildpoy	Egypt	Ida	Yerkel	Australia
Jack	Ordphin	India	Gwen	Skycard	Canada
Ken	Pastury	Peru	Holly	Vander	Kenya
Lance	Roth	China	Carol	Quinthe	Brazil

Applying clue 4, we get (in this order): Carol is Quinthe; Dolly is Nasker; Everett is Wildpoy; Freda is Thompson; Holly is Vander; Lance is Roth; Ken is Pastury; Gwen is Skycard; Jack is Ordphin; Andy is Urskel; Ida is Yerkel; Bob is Mancel.

Applying clue 5, we get (in this order): Andy Urskel, Poland; Bob Mancel, Mexico; Carol Quinthe, Brazil; Dolly Nasker, Australia; Gwen Skycard, Canada; Holly Vander, Kenya; Ida Yerkel, Australia; Freda Thompson, Spain. Everett Wildpoy, Egypt; Jack Ordphin, India; Ken Pastury, Peru; Lance Roth, China.

In the small chart accompanying the problem, the countries listed down the left side (male residents) are to be paired with those listed across the top (female residents) (6).

There are only two European countries—Poland and Spain. Poland (Andy Urskel) is paired with Australia (Dolly Nasker or Ida Yerkel) (8), and Spain (Freda Thompson) is paired with Mexico (Bob Mancel) (9). Andy isn't paired with Ida (11), so he is paired with Dolly. The other Australian (Ida Yerkel) is paired with the Egyptian (Everett Wildpoy) (8).

Then clue 7 pairs Kenya (Holly Vander) with Peru (Ken Pastury). Jack and Carol are not pen pals (10), so Jack Ordphin, India, is paired with Gwen Skycard, Canada. This leaves Lance Roth, China, paired with Carol Quinthe, Brazil.

13.

FIRST NAME	LAST NAME	FAVORITE FOOD	STATE	FAVORITE COLOR
Ada	Hill	kidney beans	Pennsylvania	umber
Brian	Farmer	lemon pie	Oregon	red
Carmella	Grey	Idaho potatoes	Nebraska	tan
Daniel	Eaton	jam	Maine	salmon

Hill is female (6) but isn't Carmella (2), so she is Ada. Her favorite color isn't red, salmon, or tan (6), so it is umber. She doesn't live in Nebraska or Oregon (1) or Maine (4, male), so she lives in Pennsylvania.

The man (4) who lives in Maine isn't Brian (4), so he is Daniel, and his last name is Eaton (1). His favorite color isn't red (7, 8) or tan (3), so it is salmon.

Carmella's favorite color isn't red (7), so it is tan, and Brian's is red. Then Carmella isn't Farmer (3, tan), so Brian is, and Carmella is Grey. Brian doesn't live in Nebraska (5, red), so Carmella does, and so Brian lives in Oregon.

The lemon pie eater is Brian (7, red). Carmella's favorite food isn't jam (2) or kidney beans (9, Nebraska), so it is Idaho potatoes. Ada Hill isn't the jam eater (2), so Daniel is, and so Ada's favorite food is kidney beans.

14.

FIRST NAME	LAST NAME	OCCUPATION
Julie	Quill	toolmaker
Kizzy	Richards	firefighter
Leon	Packard	nurse
Monty	Smith	computer operator

There are two men (1), Leon and Monty, and two women (2, 3), Julie and Kizzy. The tool maker is female (2) but isn't Kizzy (2), so she is Julie. The computer operator is male (1), so the firefighter is female (3), and so she is Kizzy. Monty isn't the nurse (5), so Leon is, and so Monty is the computer operator. Packard is male (1) but isn't Monty (1, computer operator), so he is Leon.

Richards is female (6) but isn't Julie (6), so she is Kizzy.
Quill is female (4), so she is Julie. Then Monty is Smith.